AF429070

HOW NOT TO FAIL

10 essential lessons from bringing
100 startups to market over 20 years

JEFF BERMAN

CONTENTS

To the founders and creators who make the world better
and helped me discover my purpose beyond fatherhood

* * *

*"Every journey has secret destinations of which
the traveler is unaware."* —*Martin Buber*

TOO MANY GOOD IDEAS FAIL

My mom died too young of a cancer that my doctor friends say shouldn't have killed her.

Ten years later I started working with a company that might have been able to save her life. But now I know she almost certainly would have ignored them if she'd come across them back then.

It's not that my mom didn't want to live. It's just that, like all of us, she was terrible about knowing what to notice and what to ignore. There's just too much stuff out there.

And this is the fundamental problem for anyone offering anything new. Too many good ideas fail, not because they can't create their new thing but because they can't attract the attention of the people who can put their good idea to use, even if it would help them. Even if it might save their life.

This drives me crazy.

Since 2002 I've helped more than 100 companies and not-for-profits succeed by attracting the attention of the people who can put them to use. A lot of these make people's lives better. Some have become big organizations. A few even save lives. When I can bring attention to worthwhile ideas, it feels to me like the reason why I'm on the planet.

Because smart startups shouldn't fail for stupid reasons.

MAPPING THE UNKNOWN

Imagine you're an entrepreneur. You just spent three years creating your new thing. It's been at times exhausting, ultimately exhilarating. After all the trial and error of getting it to work, you have it. It's ready.

This moment, as you're about to bring your new thing into the world, is when you're most likely to fail. And it comes as a cold shock.

After all the work of putting your thing together, you've done it. Here it is! The solution to the problem! And shockingly, no one cares. In fact, you can't even get them to pay attention long enough to see what you have.

"But wait!" you want to say. "Just look at what this is, what it can do for you! If you would just take a minute to listen, you'll see how this makes your life better! Just look!"

But they don't. Why not? What's wrong with them?

How to bring a new idea to market is the great challenge in introducing anything new, after the actual creation of the thing. Most companies fail within their first few years, and the #1 reason why is because they couldn't find a market for what they do.

Let's fix that.

Failure is the norm

The startup failure rate in 2019, the year before the pandemic, was 90%, according to the U.S. Small Business Administration. Harvard Business School says that 75% of U.S. venture-backed businesses fail. 93% of the companies accepted by YCombinator fail, according to Paul Graham, the founder of YCombinator.

All these were companies that already had a product, that had managed to create what they set out to create. And they failed. Why?

While every founder of every startup understands the challenge of creating their new thing, most don't appreciate that getting people to pause long enough to notice them is a completely separate, enormous task. And it requires a different mindset than the one they brought to the creation.

Engineer thinking vs Brand thinking

Creating any new thing is a huge challenge, filled with obstacles. Anyone who's ever done it knows how hard it is to make a new thing work, how many ways there are to get it wrong. So of course every creator puts effort into minimizing those risks.

The best way to make sure something works is to build it from things that worked before, combining them in new ways.

"Creativity is just connecting things," said Steve Jobs. "When you ask creative people how they did something, they feel a little guilty because they didn't really do it. They just saw something."

As we combine things in fresh ways to make something new, it makes sense to begin with component parts that we can count on to work.

This is the engineer's fundamental question:

Every new thing is built upon things that came before. The fewer unknown parts to contend with, the more likely the new thing will work.

Will it work? This question, the question at the foundation of creating something new, is the exact path to failure in attracting attention to the new creation.

Good engineer thinking — what makes it possible to make the new creation work — is the mindset that leads to failure in bringing any new idea to market.

Where Engineer Thinking Fails

When it comes time to take your creation to market, it's natural to apply the thinking that brought you this far, that led to the creation of your new thing.

You don't even consider there might be a problem with this method. To many creators, it seems like the only logical way to think about anything.

You look around at other successful things, and then apply what seems to work. So as you bring your new thing to market, you obviously want to use what has worked for others: what kind of message, what design, what look and feel, what media to reach the customers you imagine.

And your creation gets ignored.

Not evaluated and rejected. Just flat ignored. The people you're thinking of as customers pay zero attention to your creation, for a simple reason: because that's how our minds are wired to work.

We people, all of us, are hardwired to ignore what we've seen before.

The very thinking that guided you in creating your new thing — build upon what works — is exactly what guarantees people will ignore it now. It's not that you're doing it wrong. It's that the kind of thinking that works so well to create your new thing is making it invisible to the people you want as customers.

The Founder's Question

Getting people to pay attention to your new thing takes a different mindset, because you're actually solving a different problem. Where the engineer's question is "Will it work?", the founder's question is entirely different:

The solutions to these two questions are almost exact opposites. For the engineer, making it work is building upon what worked before. Others made something work, and their success is a good foundation for yours.

For the founder, getting anyone to care about your creation means *distinguishing* it from what else is out there. Where the engineer is happy to make it similar to what worked before, the goal of the founder is to make it different.

To succeed, you need to transition from engineer thinking to brand thinking.

Before we go further with this, let's define that word "brand", which has been randomly applied almost the point of uselessness.

"Brand" is the space you own inside people's minds.

When I say "brand" here, I'm talking about something specific: brand is whatever people are thinking about your thing. Whatever is inside people's heads that's attached to your thing, that's your brand. It's not tangible, and it's not what your creation actually does.

Your brand isn't your logo or your name or your colors or anything about how it looks or sounds or smells, although all those can help build out the space inside people's heads and give you a stronger hold in there.

Your brand is whatever people think about what you've got there.

So, if people think your thing is durable, that's part of your brand. If they say your thing is smart, that's part of your brand. If they have no thoughts, no opinion about your thing, then, no matter what you think about it or what you want others to think, you don't have a brand.

The first step toward building your brand in the minds of your (future) customers is getting them to notice it in the first place.

After creating your new thing, your biggest challenge is attracting attention to it.

As soon as we hear it, we know this is true, based upon our own experience. We are bombarded by messages from other brands trying to get our attention. Before the internet happened it was estimated there were something like 3,000 messages per day aimed at each one of us. Now the estimate is 30,000. That's messages, per day, aimed at you, me, and everyone we know with a screen.

How many new brand messages do you remember from today? Any? Of course we all walk around with deflector shields on at all times, because we're just not wired to take in that much information.

The challenge for those of us who bring new ideas to the world is that the same hard truth applies to *our* brand, even for the people we think of as our obvious customers. Even if it could save their lives.

Why is it so hard?

It's not that they're trying to be rude. When we're honest with ourselves, it's not difficult to imagine why everyone is ignoring us.

- **They are all doing something else.** Whatever the problem you can solve for people, exactly none of them are doing nothing about that now. Everyone has some solution, even if it doesn't work well, and they're not interested in hearing other ideas.

- **They're buried by 30,000 other messages.**

- **They've got other things to do.** Everyone has a life. They've got planes to catch and bills to pay, kids to pick up, reports to write, a thousand things.

- **They assume you're lying.** This is the sad, dark truth of trying to get anyone to pay attention to your thing. You're now one of 30,000 people trying to get people to notice them. The overwhelming majority of those 30,000 are a waste of time. What makes you any different?

The good news is that this is a solvable problem.

There is a system to attracting attention. I know it works, because I've been refining it over more than 20 years of working with startups, and have used it to help get more than 100 successful startups off the ground so far, create new divisions of growing companies, and even to resurrect dying brands.

Good ideas shouldn't fail for stupid reasons.

It's hard to create something new. Most inventors and innovators fail before they succeed. Pretty much everything in our lives is the result of trial and error and ultimately, something that works. (If you're interested in the history of new ideas, *How Innovation Works* by Matt Ridley is a terrific compilation of innovators' stories).

Failing to create a workable new thing is a good reason to fail. Failing to attract the attention of people who can put that worthwhile new thing to use is a terrible reason to fail.

I've seen too many good ideas disappear because the creator wasn't able to get people to try it. Often, they couldn't even get people to look at it. And that is sheer misery. To succeed in the creation and then be ignored by potential users is a gross injustice, unfair to the creator and also unfair to the world, to the people who could put the idea to use.

I'd like for that to never happen again.

— 1 —

NO ONE EAGERLY AWAITS YOUR MESSAGE.

The first step to getting people to pay attention to your new thing is to recognize that they're trying not to. The overwhelming majority of the people you're thinking of as customers are working as hard as they can to ignore you. And, as you know from your own experience on this planet, it's not that hard to ignore a new thing.

It's nice to imagine going to market as stepping up to a group of people waiting attentively to see what you've got there for them.

In reality, there's no audience waiting to hear from you. The market is a disinterested crowd of passersby, all in a hurry to get where they're going and not pausing a moment to pay attention to your creation.

Understanding this simple truth gives you a tremendous advantage over the people who run other companies and presume they have the attention of the people they want to sell to. The first step in going to market is knowing that the market does not care about you.

You have to ask yourself the founder's question: "Why should they care?"

Persuasion is alignment.

Effective persuasion is not manipulation. It's not a trick. For worthwhile creations that make the world better, this notion, that "marketing" is some kind of dark force, a necessary evil, is the opposite of the truth.

The people who will pay attention to you are the ones who believe what you believe, who share your concerns, who will resonate with why you're doing this. Once they see this truth in you, once they discover your offering comes from the same place that motivates them, they turn toward you.

Effective persuasion is when people recognize *in you* something that is important to them.

You are aligned.

This works in reverse too.

It's interesting to note that there is a flip side to this. The better aligned you are with the people you aim to serve, the less aligned you will be with people who think otherwise. And that's actually a good thing.

This is one of the most important ideas every successful founder eventually realizes. How desirable you are to someone is directly related to how undesirable you are to someone else.

Good ideas look crazy or stupid to the wrong people.

To get your thing moving, to get traction, to make someone really want it, you have to risk making someone else really *not* want it. There will always be people who turn away from you for exactly the same reasons that someone else super-loves you.

That's how this works.

And, by the way, that's not just how creating and succeeding at your startup works. That's how the whole planet is wired. For every close friend, you can think of at least one other person who just doesn't get you. And that's OK. Everyone's got their people.

With your startup, the very reason you are here is what resonates most strongly with the people you're meant to work with. What everyone else thinks does not matter, even a little bit.

Getting your brand moving means being interesting enough that someone pays attention. In the act of making yourself interesting to them, you will get the people who are *wrong* for you to notice and then turn away. That's how alignment works. It's good to see who's turned off, make sure they're not the ones you mean to turn on, and then to focus on the people you are here to serve and move forward.

But that's my Dad.

Sometimes it's hard to see people turned off by what you're doing. Especially if it's the love of your life or your Dad or that smart professor or your child or your best friend. But it's going to happen.

What to do when someone whose opinion you value tells you this is a bad idea? Ask yourself one question: Are they one of the people I'm meant to work with? Are they aligned with me on this? If they're not, even though you love them and want them to love your idea, there's an excellent chance they're just not getting it. They're not one of the people you're here to serve. You have to learn to accept their disinterest or confusion or dislike of your idea and keep your attention on the people you're meant to serve.

Every successful entrepreneur has people telling them they're crazy. And what makes it harder is that the more original and innovative the idea, the crazier it looks to the wrong people. Life is a little extra challenging when that's your lover or your Mom or your best friend. I know.

The right people will move toward you. You're attracting attention for the reason you're here. That's when you win. When the wrong people notice, they move away from your creation. And when you know it's the wrong people turning away, you know you're on the right path.

The right people are the core of your success. They're the ones who will amplify your message, carry it forward, and make your thing into a sustaining brand.

ANSWER THE QUESTION THEY'RE ALREADY ASKING.

Before the internet happened, it was estimated we were the targets of 3,000 messages per day, every day. That was in the 1990s. Now the estimate is 30,000 messages, per day, aimed at each of us. That's ridiculous.

So of course every one of us walks around trying to ignore as many messages as we can, just so we can function. And we're pretty good at it. Can you think of a single brand message from the last 24 hours? I can't. They're like gnats at a picnic.

But now, you're the one offering something new, and you're on the other side of this problem. How can you break through that wall of indifference to reach the people who can use your thing?

How can you get someone to pause long enough to even notice you?

The first step is to start with *relevance*. We pay attention to what we care about. Getting someone to listen to your message begins with delivering it to someone who shares the same concerns, someone who would understand why you're doing this in the first place, someone who has a problem you can solve.

Who cares?

Most of the messages we encounter are irrelevant to our concerns. It's easy to ignore them when they have nothing to do with us.

Now, when you turn it around to think about how to attract the attention of the people you want to serve, you want to consider the world from their point of view.

Most people with a problem are so focused on their situation, they have a hard time lifting their gaze to notice an unexpected solution.

In fact, there's a challenging paradox here: the more original your solution — the more innovative it is — the harder it is to get people to pay attention to it. This has to do with human psychology and the way our attention is wired, which we'll discuss in more detail in Chapter 4.

How do you get their attention? You meet them where they are.

If a potential user sees that you understand how their problem looks from their perspective, they start to see you as an ally, as someone worth paying attention to.

You can actually watch this happen in real life when people encounter a new idea that rings true. Their eyes widen and you can see them start to nod their heads in agreement. They recognize a like-minded thinker. You're expressing the same concerns they have. And then you have a chance of getting them to see what you've got here.

Notice, we're not talking about your thing yet.

We're not saying anything about what it does or how it works or anything about it. The focus is entirely on the person who can use it. If you put yourself in the mindset of a potential user, you have a much better chance of being in tune with their thoughts. Suddenly, you're relevant to their concerns. And that gives you a better chance of breaking through the barrier they set up between themselves and anything new.

It's not about your thing yet.

There's one big challenge, and I've seen this with pretty much every founder I've worked with, including (maybe especially) myself: You have to turn your own brain off. You need to stop thinking about your thing for a moment.

It sounds simple, but this is one of the most difficult things to do. It's hard to stop thinking about what you have to offer, right as you're offering it. "Not thinking about my creation? That's why I'm *here*." But what matters in this moment isn't what you created, but the mindset of your potential user.

Here's a thought exercise that helps:

You need to see your offering as a thing separate from yourself. People who practice meditation learn to see their thoughts and feelings as something apart from themselves. This is something like that. You want to see your offering as its own thing, separate from you, maybe from a little distance.

Step back from it. It's still there. You can turn away from it, and back, to check. See? Still there, ready for whatever you're going to do next.

Now, turn to the side a little, away from your creation, and turn to your prospective user, who doesn't yet know anything about what you have to offer. Just look at this potential customer.

It helps to have a specific person in mind, someone you know, someone you can visualize. Try to focus on a real person. Maybe pull up a picture of her or him or them. Get a clear notion of that person. And then ask yourself these questions:

- Who is this person?

- How do they think about their problem? What do they want?

- What are they doing about that now?

- How's that working out for them? What's working? What's not?

- What would they like to do if they could?

Put yourself in the mindset of this person, *before* you say anything about what you have to offer. You're not trying to persuade them of anything yet. You're just trying to understand them from the inside. The better you can see how the world looks from their perspective, the better you can create a message that aligns with their thinking.

It ain't you.

Founders often tell me, "That's easy. I know exactly who this is for and how they think, because they're exactly like me! As long as I do what solves my problem, I'm solving it for everyone like me. That's easy."

Yes, it's true, you're the first and most important user. And every user to follow may be almost exactly like you. Except for one thing:

They didn't just spend three years living and breathing life into this thing you're making. They may share all your concerns but they'll never have your perspective. The act of creating your thing changed you. Now you need to dial your mindset back to where it was when you got started.

How does someone think who has all your concerns but hasn't yet solved them? You have to forget what you know. You have to get back to the beginner's mind.

Pacing and Leading

Psychologists' term for what we're doing here is *pacing and leading*. Before you put anything new to a prospective user, you want to make clear that you understand them, that you're in tune with how they think, that you care about the same things they care about. Creating a message that's relevant to their concerns begins with understanding this person, how the problem or opportunity or need or desire looks and feels from their point of view.

You want them to lean toward you, to opt in.

Engagement is much more powerful than interruption. No one likes being interrupted in the middle of whatever they're doing to listen to something new. Interruption messages are notoriously unsuccessful.

You know this from your own life. And the internet is learning it too. As I write this, on average only 1 of every 217 online ads results in a click. This is why websites are moving away from interruption advertising and into subscriptions. Interruption is a dumb business model.

Engagement works on exactly the opposite principle. If we can engage people by helping them solve a problem, meet a need, satisfy a desire, we have an exponentially greater chance of being heard, being remembered, and tilting them toward *yes*.

A story about answering the right question

When Wikipedia first became a thing, the people most excited about it were students on university campuses.

Until then, anyone writing a paper needed to do a fair amount of work to find reference sources. This meant going to the library, finding the right books or journals and taking careful note of the authors and publishers to cite in their work.

Wikipedia made all that seem unnecessary. Now, anyone could just do an online search on whatever topic they were writing about and, bam, a whole page of material popped up. A lot of research papers were showing up citing Wikipedia sources.

Suddenly, librarians and libraries seemed like a waste of time.

Not so fast

But there was a problem. Wikipedia articles could be written and edited by anyone, and (at the time) had no accreditation.

A lot of sketchy information was finding its way into student work, which is the opposite of what academic research is supposed to be about. Wikipedia was enabling a generation of work based upon unverified sources, which meant academic research was increasingly built on sand. University faculty were not happy.

Does the old school matter?

Who else was not happy were the publishers of respected sources, such as Grey's Anatomy and the Oxford English Dictionary and Encyclopedia Brittanica. They saw how research was changing and were pretty sure they were at risk of becoming irrelevant. They wanted to remain the sources students looked to when they did their research.

To maintain their place as the authority on defining words, the Oxford English Dictionary needed to be accessible to students searching with digital tools. They were afraid the OED would end up a big cumbersome book up on a shelf, while university students, and increasingly, professors, defaulted to easy online sources.

Bringing reliable sources to digital search

Right around this time, some smart, forward-thinking librarians got together with some talented software engineers to solve this problem. They signed up many of the best big authoritative publishers, put all their content into a big database, and made it all interconnected and searchable.

Everything across dozens of the most important reference works could now be found in one place.

So a search for "Galileo" would bring up a biography of the Renaissance scientist from the *Cambridge Dictionary of Philosophy*, as well as an article on the Galilean satellites of Jupiter from *Philip's Atlas of the Universe*, and a detailed description of Galileo's trial in *The Bridgeman Art Library Archive*. All this was easy to find, easy to attribute, and cross-referenced.

The Naming Trap

When it came time to name this creation, the people who built it decided the name should answer a simple question: How does this new invention work?

They decided to name it based on what they saw as its primary feature: all these great, important books are now all cross-referenced in one place.

They named their company X-Refer, which to them was clear shorthand for "cross-referenced," and they took their creation to universities and big public libraries so these great sources could again be accessible.

And nobody cared.

What happened? Why weren't the librarians and the university administrators excited about this wonderful new way to bring students and faculty back to solid, creditable sources?

Because, in naming their creation X-Refer, the founders were answering the wrong question. Almost no one cared how the new solution works. The founders came to the naming task assuming people would look at their creation and ask, "What is this? What do you have there?"

The problem was that the creators didn't have anyone's attention yet. It's impossible to persuade someone who's walking away from you.

As they suffered the indifference of their intended users, they reached out to me and my team to rename and rebrand this good idea, to make research meaningful again.

Answer the question they're already asking

We began our work with X-Refer by asking fundamental questions and discussing the answers with the X-Refer team.

- Who are the people you want to attract?

- How do they think about their problem?

- What are they doing about that now?

- What would they like to do if they could?

As Wikipedia and Google became the default for how people on campus conduct research, librarians and university decision makers faced a growing problem with credibility. Wikipedia articles could be written by anyone, often with nothing backing them up. It turns out the internet is a font of unreliable information.

The librarians and university decision makers that X-Refer wanted as clients needed something that combined the ease of use of Google with the authority of Grey's Anatomy.

The mission follows the vision.

With this strategy clear and agreed, we set out to rename the company.

We did three rounds of name generation and discussion, considering hundreds of options. The result was a name that answers the question their desired users were already asking:

Is there a creditable version of Wikipedia?

Beyond the word 'Credo', the visual brand identity alludes to the long history of reference materials, from classical times through the Renaissance to the torrent of modern works, with an unsubtle nod to copyright, as opposed to what a researcher might find online.

Within one year, Credo Reference became the leading and then the default solution for providing authoritative, credible, digital search tools to universities.

One way to create an ad is to pick a bully. The internet makes a good bully.

What changed was how the company looked to its prospective users, the librarians and acquisitions people at colleges and universities, the people searching for a way to get their students back to reliable, creditable research sources.

The name Credo Reference looked like the answer to the question they were already asking.

Once their prospects' interest was piqued, the solution sold itself. The company founders learned they needed to attract their prospects' attention before they could explain anything about their solution.

$$- \mathbf{3} -$$

YOU'VE GOT A BETTER MESSAGE THAN 'HOW IT WORKS'.

A few years ago, I was hired to work with a struggling startup. This is the company I mention in the introduction to the book, the one that might have been able to save my Mom's life.

They were the first to offer a working system for remote medical care in the U.S., and they weren't getting traction. They'd been at it for 15 years, scrambling to find customers among the big employers they needed to make be profitable.

They were thinking about pulling out of the U.S. entirely.

Advance Medical had figured out a way to dramatically improve healthcare by helping each patient connect with the doctor most expert in that patient's specific disease.

Before they came along, any diagnosis of any health issue depended just on the knowledge and experience of the doctor in the room with the patient. That might be fine for common problems, or in a big hospital with many experts who can be brought in to consult on something out of the ordinary.

But our bodies can go wrong in so many different ways. There are more than 10,000 diseases that go under the label 'cancer'. If you're suffering from something strange, the odds that your local doctor can diagnose it and figure out how to treat you are really low. Most people don't have access to the leading experts in their particular problem.

Then the internet happened, which made it possible for medical records to be shared much more easily than before. Soon, healthcare regulations caught up with the technology, and experts who were not in same the room as patients — or even in the same country — could now consult on anything and help recommend treatments. Which meant the leading expert in any patient's given condition could be made part of the healthcare team, if the connection could be made.

Advance Medical solved exactly this problem.

Building on their own medical knowledge and connections, their physicians and technologists created a network of medical experts on virtually every medical condition. Suddenly, it was possible for patients to connect directly with the specialists best able to diagnose and treat their specific condition, even if the patient and specialists were nowhere near each other.

It was a kind of matchmaking system, but instead of dating, it matched healthcare experts with the people who most needed them. Patients benefitted by getting the most expert care. Specialists benefitted by applying their expertise where it's most useful. It seemed like this was what advanced healthcare should be. Win-win.

Except Advance Medical was failing. After an encouraging early start, sales were almost non-existent. Only a few of the big companies targeted by Advance Medical were interested in adding this benefit. After years of trying and failing to get market traction, the leadership of Advance Medical was thinking of pulling up stakes in the U.S.

What was wrong?

In their eagerness to share their breakthrough program with the people who could put it to use, Advance Medical spent their time and money talking all about how it worked. And, it turns out, that 'How It Works' message was invisible to almost everyone Advance Medical was trying to attract.

"How It Works" messages are powerful early on and ineffective soon after.

This simple truth explains why many companies crash so soon after seeing early success. The message that helps startups get traction early is the exact thing that leads to their failure soon after. And most never understand why.

Most people who bring a new idea to market start off by thinking of "the market" as a big, undifferentiated mass of people that includes a subset of the people who might be interested in their new thing.

But your market isn't a giant blob of faceless people. Your potential users fit into distinct groups who respond to new ideas differently.

Who your potential users are and how they'll respond to your creation can be predicted in advance. The technology adoption curve, described in detail by Geoffrey Moore in Crossing The Chasm, explains the power and the failure of 'How It Works' messages in bringing new ideas to market.

The Technology Adoption Curve

For any innovation, we can divide the potential market into five discrete groups. The key is that these groups think differently from each other, have different attitudes to new ideas, and respond to different types of messages.

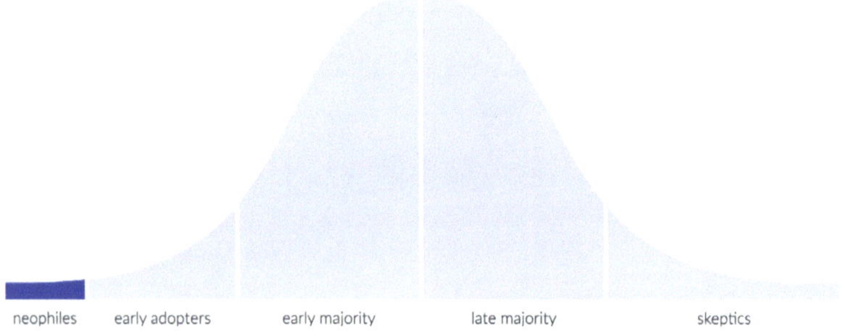

Neophiles are attracted to anything new in the subject they care about.

Neophiles want to learn what's the latest thing, how it works, what it does well and what it doesn't. Whether or not it actually does what it says it does is just part of the overall news for people like this. They're drawn to the newness of it.

We all know people like this, the ones who try the latest gadget and then love talking about what they've learned, comparing notes with other enthusiasts and sharing their thoughts with the rest of us. If it works, great. If not, that's no great loss to the neophiles. They're more interested in learning about the next thing than in solving a specific problem or meeting a specific need. And if they have a real need and the new thing doesn't quite cut it, they've got seven other gadgets to try on it.

It's worth noting that a given person might be a neophile in one area and something completely different elsewhere. Someone attracted to all the latest kitchen gadgets may have a very different mindset when it comes to cars, or vice versa. Any activity with new ideas comes with its own set of neophiles.

For anyone bringing something new to market, these neophiles are a great place to get early feedback and thoughts on what might make the new thing better. Neophiles love to share thoughts on their enthusiasms and are happy to be in touch with the creators of the latest thing.

But don't expect to build a market on them. Even if your thing is perfect and does its job beautifully, the neophiles will give you thumbs up and then move onto the next new thing. They're fickle; often interested but rarely loyal.

It's important to keep in mind these first users are no more than 1% to 2% of your total market opportunity. They're great to talk with but not so much to build the foundation

for a sustaining business. Because neophiles love learning and sharing what they've learned, they can play a part in attracting your next, much larger set of prospects.

Early Adopters are the users who first pick up your new thing to solve a specific problem. These people are smart and think deeply about their needs, to the point where they can imagine what a solution might look like. They recognize your new thing as a possible answer to the question they've been asking.

In fact, they understand their problem so well that they can connect a How It Works message with their need. They're moving through the world with picture in their mind of what a possible solution might look like.

Your Early Adopters actually envision your solution much as you did before you created it. When they see your actual thing, they recognize it. It rings true to them.

There's a beautiful resonance between creators and Early Adopters. You share the same vision.

Because you and your Early Adopters have both spent time thinking about the problem, you're in sync before you find each other. Early Adopters know it may not be easy to solve their problem, and they appreciate the work that goes into creating the new solution.

Early Adopters have a defined need, so they're more demanding than the Neophiles who came before. They want your thing to work and they will let you know if it doesn't. They're smart and capable and are often willing to work with creators to iron out performance wrinkles to get the new thing working the way they need it to.

If your thing solves their problem better than what came before, Early Adopters are super appreciative of that early on. Once you have it working right, they can become your greatest evangelists, spreading the word of your new thing to the broader market. So making them happy pays dividends beyond the initial sale. You're creating a set of enthusiastic advocates for your brand.

Early Adopters are about 13% of your total market opportunity.

And that's everyone who cares about how your thing works.

Together, these first two groups, the Neophiles and Early Adopters, represent about 15% of the potential market for a new product, roughly 1 of every 7 people across the total market. Your Neophiles and Early Adopters include pretty much everyone interested in how the new thing works.

All your potential customers outside these first early buyers don't have the imagination to picture what a solution to their problem might look like.

This explains why your How It Works messages are likely to fail in the long term.

How this played out for Advance Medical

Advance Medical was failing because their message was all about Advance Medical, what it does and how it works. And, for most of their potential customers, that made their message invisible.

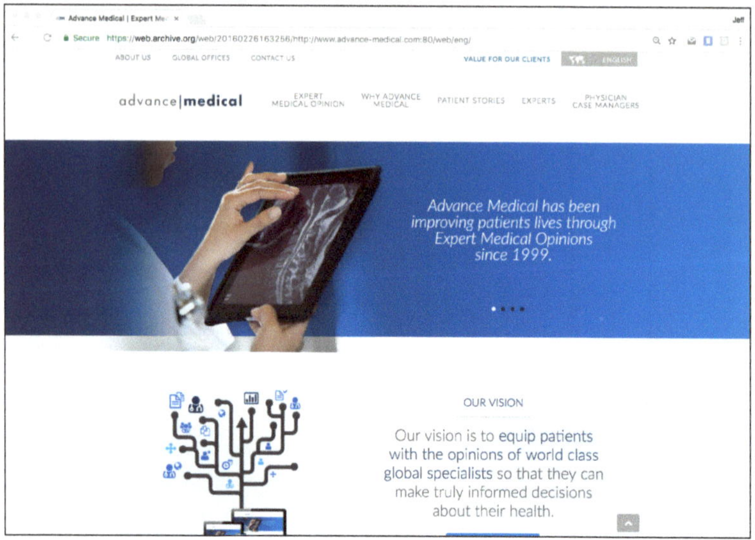

This was not a good website. It had nothing to do with anything anyone cared about.

Almost every startup I've worked with builds its initial marketing around How It Works. It's easy to understand why.

They just spent years creating their new thing. They're focused on it, and proud of their accomplishment. Many founders are engineers, or doctors, or scientists who work hard to create something that didn't exist before. Of course they're proud of it. Now they're finally ready to show it to the world.

They assume the questions on everyone's mind are something like, "What have you got there? How does it work?"

And, for the first people interested, it actually works something like that. The Neophiles and Early Adopters are the first ones in, and they really do want to hear what it does and how it works. These first customers want to open the hood and look at the engine. They're happy poking at the innards like judges at a science fair. They come closest to sharing the founder's enthusiasm for how this new thing solves an old problem. They're the ones most likely to give the new idea the admiration it deserves.

It's at this point where startups falter, and most fail.

After attracting early interest from enthusiasts, founders and investors get excited and ramp up marketing spend, to grow their market and see a return on their investment. They take the message that worked with their early users and bring it to the wider market. And the wider market ignores them.

What happens? Why doesn't the early success just scale up?

The problem is that the Neophiles and Early Adopters, who care about how it works, are very different from the much larger group that comes next.

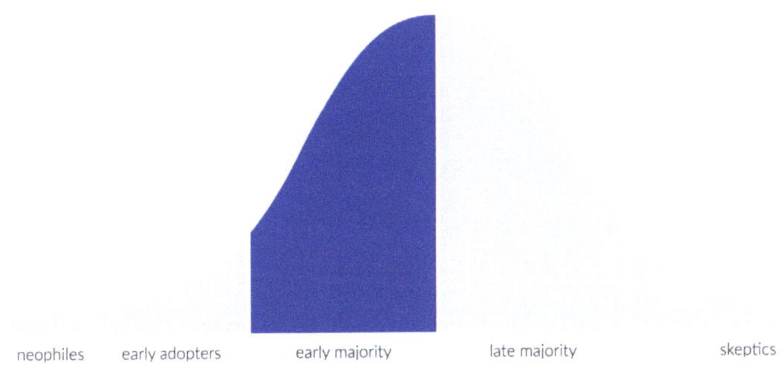

The Early Majority is where companies become sustainable brands. And while they have problems similar to the problems of Early Adopters, their decision-making process is completely different.

The Early Majority represents more than one-third of your total market opportunity, about 34% of all your prospects, more than twice as many as the Neophiles and Early Adopters combined. And, in addition to being a bigger crowd of people, they're a lot more loyal than either of the early groups. You can build a real business serving these people's needs.

But there's a catch. The Early Majority have a problem to solve similar to the problems of the Early Adopters. But where the Early Adopters can envision what a solution to their problem might look like, the Early Majority cannot.

They just don't have the imagination to picture a solution.

The Early Majority is just as focused on their problem as the Early Adopters, maybe even more so. They are honed in on it. To them, the problem is everything. The challenge is that the Early Majority is so focused on their problem, they can't pick up their heads to envision a solution. They may be wary of disrupting how things are done, tied to their current systems and processes. The Early Majority includes a lot of people who are wary of breaking the rules.

Because they can't imagine what a solution might look like, they don't have a picture in their minds of something like your thing. They don't think that way, and so they don't spend time wondering how such a thing might work.

They're so stuck on their problem, they literally can't see the solution. The answer could be put right in front of their face, but they won't see it.

So a How It Works message makes no sense to the Early Majority. Your How It Works message is literally invisible to them. The Early Majority simply cannot connect your How It Works message with the problem they're so focused on. They're stuck.

This is why startups that scale up following the early success of their How It Works marketing often find themselves on the brink of failure soon afterward. They spend money and time delivering a message to a group of people *who need their product* but aren't capable of hearing their message.

This is astonishing. Here are two people: one who has a clear need, the other who has a solution and is telling the needy one how it works, and the needy one turns away.

What can be done?

— **4** —

ATTENTION IS NOT RATIONAL.

Of everything I've learned over my work with dozens of companies about how go to market actually works and how to create a system to solve it, this is the most difficult thing I've had to learn and the most difficult thing to teach. It took me years to understand why this is true and what it means for coming up with and delivering an effective message.

The simple truth is that, for everyone outside the 15% who make up your Neophile and Early Adopter customers — in other words, for 6 of every 7 of your possible customers — explaining why they should want your thing, using reasons, appealing to logic, does not work.

I know that sounds crazy.

Why it's true is explained in a Nobel Prize-winning book that is fascinating, dense, filled with insight, and twice as long as it needs to be. To be honest, I empathize with Daniel Kahneman's editor. I wouldn't want to be in the position of telling anyone this smart to shave his content in half. Kahneman was a brilliant and important thinker. His groundbreaking book is called Thinking Fast and Slow.

Kahneman, along with his late partner Amos Twersky, created what is now known as behavioral economics, although their core work is in psychology. Before they came along, economics didn't take into account how people make decisions, which is a big reason why economists so often get things wrong. It's pretty wild and humbling to think that economics, for two centuries, was based entirely on the "rational man" theory that's now almost entirely disproven, with real experiments to back up the findings. We humans have still got a lot to learn about ourselves.

Fundamentally, Kahneman and Twersky figured out — applying the scientific method, with experiments and testable hypotheses — how human decision making works. It's an important book.

There are dozens of fascinating revelations on how our minds work in *Thinking Fast and Slow.* Let's focus on the insights that have to do with bringing your brand to market.

We think of ourselves as rational, making decisions as they come up by using experience and logic to arrive at the best answer. "I will look at the advantages and disadvantages of each option and then decide on the best course of action," is something like what we tell ourselves.

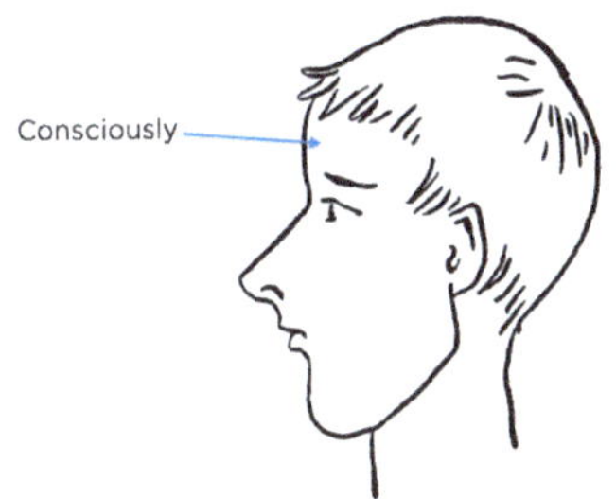

What Kahneman shows is that there are simply too many decisions for us to make in any given moment for decision making to work this way. In a series of brilliant experiments, Kahneman and Twersky more or less proved their hypothesis that the human mind operates by running two systems simultaneously.

What we think of as our conscious selves they call System Two. It's the part of us that's reading this book, knows the complementary color of yellow (indigo, on the other side of the color wheel), and that the capital of Massachusetts is Boston and the capital of Illinois isn't Chicago but Springfield (the Springfield in Illinois, not the one in Massachusetts or the one on the Simpsons).

System Two is the part of ourselves that we think of as our 'self'. It's our self-awareness, the conscious part, the part that we think is doing the decision making.

The other part of our minds, System One, is the pre-conscious part. It's the part that works as a filter on the world.

System One is what keeps our bodies working, doing the breathing, making sure we're not about to be attacked, telling us when we're hungry or tired, and answering the easiest questions for us without much effort (simple math like 2 + 2, reading short words, noting whether we should push or pull that door).

System One is the fast-thinking part of our brains, the part that we're mostly not aware of. System Two is the slow-thinking part of our brains that does the focused, effortful work.

There's a clear evolutionary reason why we're wired this way. Our brains are the most expensive organ we run — energy-wise — sucking up 30% of the glucose we use every minute in spite of being only about 2% of our body weight. So our brains are always trying to avoid unnecessary work. This isn't laziness; it's resource management. (By the way, this is a powerful comeback to accusations of slacking. "I'm not lazy. I'm conserving resources.")

System One continually runs interference for System Two, to avoid unnecessary work. If System One decides something is not worth our focused attention it tells System Two to ignore it, saving the energy for the hard stuff.

So what kind of thing does System One decide is not worth our focused attention? Virtually everything.

This is not an exaggeration. There is so much information flowing through our senses at any given point, we would overload and shut down if we tried to pay attention to it all. System One evolved to allow us to function. It lets through only the most urgent or most interesting or most threatening information.

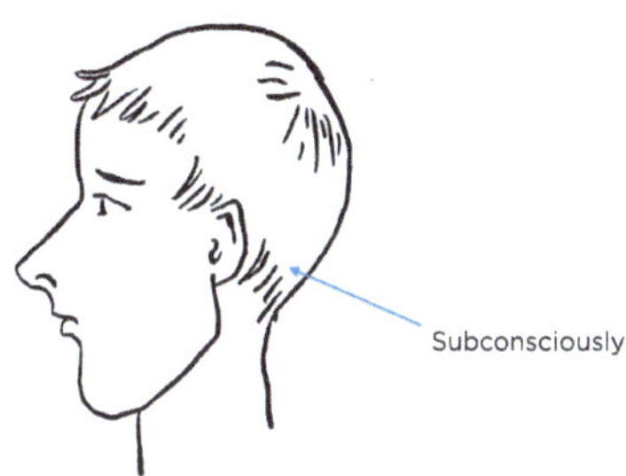

Which is why I (and probably you) don't remember a single one of the 30,000 or so messages directed at us today. My System One shut them out. It's the part of my brain that says, "I ain't got time for that."

Now, this is the problem we face as creators: If you have something to offer someone, something new, something worthwhile, maybe even something that would *save their life*, how do you get through?

This is the great challenge of bringing a new thing to market, and understanding it is the beginning of getting to the answer. Everyone you're trying to reach has a built-in System One filter that will not allow you enough of their attention to explain why they should want, or even consider, your thing. You can't get a foot in the door to tell them what's so great. So what can you do?

You have to make them want it before they know why they want it.

This is the simple truth that's so difficult to act on. You need to figure out how to build the *want* upfront, before you've had a chance to explain anything.

Some brands have tried to shortcut the attention deficit problem by tricking us into paying attention by using sex or death to make us watch. We've all seen ads that cloak their message in something difficult to ignore, something terrifying or arousing, to trick System One into showing the message to System Two.

This doesn't work.

The problem with the tricks of terror or sex is that System Two is not stupid. Once the terrifying or sexy message gets through System One and is recognized as not dangerous and not a path to getting laid, our System Two sees it has been played and turns off the message. And once System Two recognizes a lie, it doesn't reward the liar with any attention in the future. System Two is good at holding onto a grudge.

You can't easily trick people into paying attention.

So the *want* you build into the front of your message needs to line up with what you have to offer. You have to make them want it before they know why they want it, and that *want* has to ring true to why you're here.

Solving the attention deficit forces us to do the hard work of understanding where our thing aligns with the needs, concerns, desires, or dreams of the people we want as customers.

That's the work.

Reframing Advance Medical

In creating a new message for Advance Medical, we knew we needed to move away from their old How It Works message and turn our attention to the people they were trying to attract. The insight for how to do this came from answering two questions:

1. How do the people they want as customers — in this case, enterprise HR Directors, the ones making decisions about HR benefits in big companies — think about their problem?

2. Why was Advance Medical created to begin with?

The answer came once we stopped thinking of HR Directors as potential buyers and started thinking of them as people. Every one of these HR Directors knew someone who had a health crisis. For many, it was a senior member of their company. For others, a member of their own family, or the family of someone they work with. Some had critical health issues themselves.

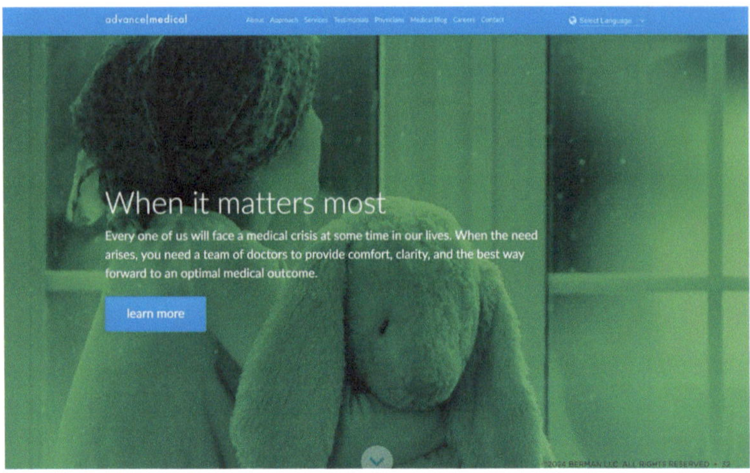

Make them want it before they know why they want it.

When we spoke with the Advance Medical leadership about why they created the company in the first place, their reason shone through. They personally knew doctors, experts at specific conditions, who were struggling to connect with patients suffering from exactly that disease. And they knew of patients who were misdiagnosed, undertreated, or mistreated simply because they hadn't connected with the most knowledgeable experts.

The value of what Advance Medical does went from an abstraction to an immediate, obvious blessing.

Every one of us will face a medical crisis at some time in our lives. When the need arises, you need a team of doctors to provide comfort, clarity, and the best way forward to an optimal medical outcome.

Once we framed the message to make it personal, it cut right through the System One filter. As with the best insights, the answer seemed obvious once we had it. Because we were able to express this clearly and in simple terms, it was easily remembered and shared by everyone who worked at Advance Medical and everyone who worked with them. The message had legs.

After updating their website, we moved on to refreshing Advance Medical's print materials, working with their sales team on coordinating the sales and marketing messages to build upon each other. The reframe inspired Advance Medical to create a new set of services: Virtual Medical Homes dedicated to connecting experts with underserved patient populations and those with rare or exceptional 'orphan' diseases.

Focusing Advance Medical's message energized the entire organization. Everyone in the company now knew what made them worthwhile and why their work was important. Customers, partners, and employees understood the value and were eager to share it. Within two years they went from struggling to leading the category, ultimately leading to a successful merger with Teledoc.

They succeeded because they had a message that attracted attention for the reason they exist.   That message made people want it before they knew why they wanted it.

THINK OF YOUR CREATION AS THE TANGIBLE EXPRESSION OF A DEEPER VALUE.

Your first and most difficult task in bringing your idea to market is getting someone to pause whatever they're doing long enough to notice you. How to make that happen begins with framing how you think about your offer.

Instead of a product or a service or really any kind of *thing*, you can create a more compelling message by thinking of your creation as coming from a deeper place. At its core, your thing is not a thing at all. It's the tangible expression of a strongly held belief.

Because you hold this value, you created this thing.

Because Advance Medical believes every patient should have access to the best medical expert on their condition, they created these services.

Because you hold these values, you created this thing. This is the key to attracting attention from people who are trying to ignore you.

How Nike went from selling running shoes to defining athletic performance

Back in the day when running became a thing everyone wanted to do, Nike was in the lead for what you wore on your feet. They were a running shoe company. That's how they talked about themselves and that's how they were understood.

In the beginning, Nike's advertising was as dull as anyone's.

At the time, I was a teenager working in a store and selling a lot of Nike shoes. That was going well, so Nike sent us some apparel they'd just created, shorts and shirts and shiny track suits.

We put those clothes right out there next to the running shoes. And they just sat there. People would come in, see the shirts and hoodies, and laugh. "Why would I buy a *jacket* from a *shoe* company?" It made no sense to them. Nike was a running shoe company.

It's hard to imagine now. Anything that wasn't about running from Nike seemed crazy, off-brand, like walking into a drugstore and seeing M&Ms toothpaste. It just came off *wrong*. After three months of not moving much Nike apparel, we sent it back.

And then Nike shifted the frame away from their products and onto their purpose.

Because Nike believes in the soul of the athlete, they create these products. Messaging on their values, and not only the things they're selling, gave them permission to stretch beyond running shoes and now into anything athletic.

Nike reshaped the category when they stopped talking about shoes and started talking about why they're here. Many of the "Just Do It" ads don't mention shoes at all. They focus on the athletes, and more deeply: on what makes this particular athlete exceptional. By putting their core values up front, Nike connected with everyone who shared those values. The reaction to their messaging went from something like, "Hmm, nice shoes," to something like, "Hell yeah."

Where's the Nike product in this ad?

In every category you can think of, the market leader has built its values into the heart of their message. What's worth noting is the order of those things happening.

Before I studied this, my assumption was that Nike, and every major brand, became the big player first and then started talking about their values. That's not what happened. The focus on values came after they had built a user base but long before they became the category leader.

There's a consistent arc to how dominant brands' messages evolve. They begin by serving the product enthusiasts and their messages reflect this focus, talking almost exclusively about what they make and how it works.

The leap happens when they consider the concerns of possible users beyond their early adopters.

Elevation vs dumbing down

The risk is thinking that the appeal to the broader market, that first move into your Early Majority, involves dumbing down the message, that it represents some kind of sellout, that it undermines the purity of your brand.

To early enthusiasts, it can feel this way. "I was into them before they were cool," we hear about a band or clothing brand once they make their move to a wider audience.

To the creators who know why they're doing what they're doing, the size of the audience is secondary. What matters is whether they're true to their vision. Most of them want to reach more people. But the meaning of the connection is at the heart of their growth. The growth is a function of their meaning.

Building your message around why you're here makes it possible to connect with people who share your vision but don't necessarily understand how it works. You're resonating with them at a deeper level than features or function. When you make your purpose clear, you elevate your brand among people with similar values.

Nike didn't start with "Just do it"

This is not to suggest you go out to find your version of "Just do it" and make that the focus of your message as you first go to market. Before you can inspire anyone, they need to know what you have to offer.

In bringing out anything new, it's important to keep in mind how new products move through the market. (See Chapter 3.) Your first customers are the ones who are interested in how your new thing works and what it does. Every successful brand begins this way, including Nike.

You start there, and then take their enthusiasm into the larger early majority.

Remember why you got started

Even as you bring your creation to your first users, talking about features and functions and how it works, your messages should resonate with why you got started on this to begin with. The thing that drove you to create is something every one of your users will recognize as true.

Ultimately, this is what separates you from everyone else.

When your creation embodies the values at the heart of it, when you're clear about the need you meet and how you meet it, your potential customers recognize and turn toward the message.

— 6 —

DESIGN IS A FORCE MULTIPLIER.

Think of any brand you love. When you see something from that brand, the one thing that shines through consistently is the love of the creator, their enthusiasm for what they made. They've built their love into it, into the DNA of the thing and into every expression of it. It's right there.

This is the power of design. It's not a trick to make someone notice. The creator's reason why is built into everything about it.

Attention. Please.

The first step to getting someone to take an interest in your thing is getting them to notice it.

And that's hard to do. Because we know, whatever your creation does, the people you want to attract are all doing something else about to meet that need now. No one is going around with a need entirely unfulfilled, waiting around for someone to create some way to solve it.

Everyone is already doing something else. And what's worse, and even more frustrating: Even if their current solution is mediocre, people are mostly unwilling to consider something new.

It's frustrating. But if you think about it, it makes sense. There are just too many things we all have to do every day for us to consider alternatives. We default to what we have now, not because we're delighted with how it works but because it's generally not worth the trouble to investigate alternatives. Most of them are a waste of time anyway. If we were continually exploring better solutions for everything, we'd never have time to do anything else.

So we shrug and accept suboptimal solutions because it's easier than checking out something new. Until the new thing becomes impossible to ignore.

Now you're the new thing.

Once you create your new thing, a better way to do something, your task is to make it so compelling to your intended users that they cannot ignore it. They absolutely have to check it out, even though they're busy, even though they're doing something else, even though they're not actively looking for a better idea.

So how do you get them to pause long enough to notice you and pay you some of their precious attention?

Design shows what you put into this.

By design, I don't mean the wrapper. Design isn't a bow you put on top of your thing to make it pretty. As Steve Jobs said, "Design isn't how it looks. Design is how it works."

Done well, design can change everything about how someone thinks about your thing, by reframing their thinking to get them to see it not as an acceptable alternative but as an entirely new and better answer to their problem.

Good design gives you the power to change people's thinking even before they know they're thinking at all. Done well, design is a shortcut to bypass the System One perception filters that all your potential users run, 24/7.

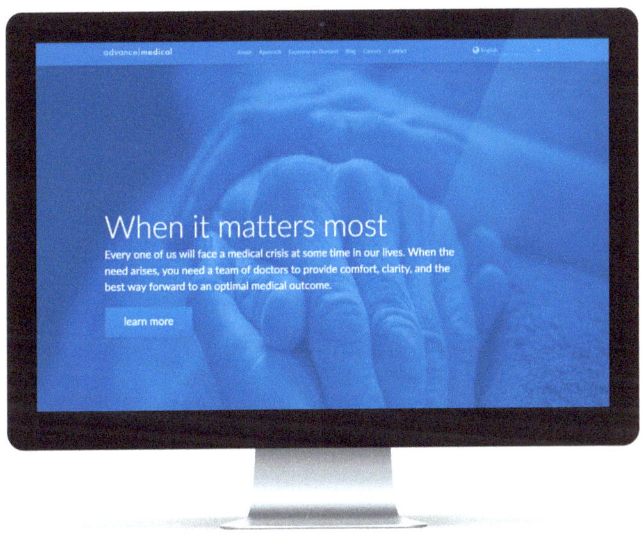

Before we read the words, we see the image. We used images of hands touching hands to emphasize how Advance Medical facilitates the one-to-one doctor-patient relationship, framing Advance Medical as a way to improve the essential person-to-person foundation of medical care.

See what I mean?

We're visual creatures from the start. It's hardwired. Before they become eyeballs, our eyes start out as brain cells. A few specific neurons of ours start to differentiate themselves from the rest of our gray matter before we're born to be light-sensitive carriers of information from the outside world.

Which, from an evolution perspective, makes sense. From the very beginning, if we humans were going to survive long enough to grow up and have children and keep our species going, we were going to need to know where are the predators and where is the food and water and which is the person we'd like to make the babies with. Eyes are essential to our success. So we're constantly scanning our environment for threats and opportunities.

From a founder's perspective, now that you have something worthwhile to offer the world you can use this system to attract attention to your good idea.

Using the power of the visual stupidly

Of course, people have always taken advantage of images as a shortcut to attract our attention. Because we're wired to notice threats and mating opportunities, dangerous and sexy images get to skip the line when our System One perception filters prioritize information for our System Two thinking brains.

Is the Challenger the sports car that offers a lady a place to put on the rest of her clothes? Or are we about to witness some kind of Transformers fantasy here? The problem is that we remember the lady and forget the car.

That kind of thing might work once and then never again. Buyers don't like being fooled, and those who take advantage of us generally get labeled as liars and not rewarded with our attention next time.

Good design embodies the values of your creation.

When you're clear in your own mind on what your thing is about, why it's here, you can use design to attract the right people to it.

At a time when every other car maker in the U.S. was about size, VW invited buyers to think differently. People who care about the history of advertising consider this the first modern advertising campaign.

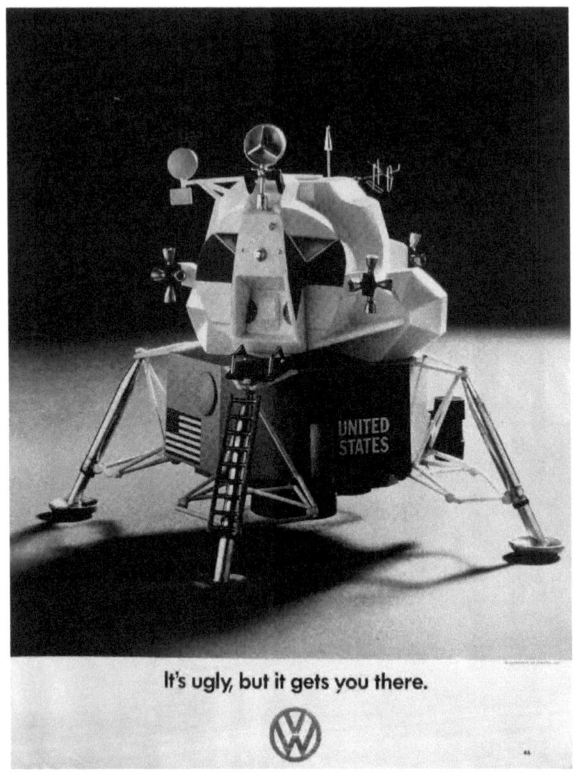

Then, a few years later, VW did this. What's especially wonderful: it shows an iconic vehicle that's not a Volkswagen and has no Volkswagen parts. But it embodies the values at the heart of every VW and every VW buyer.

As the car world got practical, the people behind the Corvette stepped up to own the idea of the car as something more than a way to get from point A to point B. Corvette is an icon because car lovers know why it exists. The Corvette still embodies the values that led to its creation more than 70 years ago.

Know yourself.

The key to using design to your advantage is to first get clear in your own mind what you stand for. What are the core values at the heart of your creation?

Without overthinking it, what are three adjectives that describe why you're here? Write them down. It's OK to take some time to hone this thinking, because this is the very center of how you express yourself to the people you imagine as buyers.

What are you about?

Here's a thought exercise to get started. Sit quietly for a moment, and think of your creation as a person. It could even be you, or someone you know.

If you had to choose one single attribute, one descriptor, one personality trait to describe your creation, what is it?

DoorDash wants you to think *speed*. So when they started delivering for McDonald's, they announced it by showing the Big Mac, in motion.

Be who you are.

As you build your vision, create your user experience and your message, how well are you expressing the core attributes of your brand? A brand that embodies *zen* probably wants to present itself differently than one that's all about *breakthrough*. There's no such thing as a universal positive attribute.

When your values align with how you appear in the world, your future users have an easier time getting a handle on what you are. They will be attracted to your creation for the very reasons it exists.

And then your users themselves become a part of how future users understand your brand values. Your future users are attracted to your early adopters. They see themselves in those people.

This is the key to attracting the attention of strangers. Design is the quickest window into the soul of your brand.

— 7 —

COMPANIES DON'T MAKE DECISIONS. PEOPLE DO.

You can't sell anything to an organization. You need to find someone inside there who has the problem your creation solves. Then you can work on attracting that person's attention.

Let's say your creation solves a problem for someone inside a company. That's great, because people can decide to work with you, and then you have a business.

To make it work, though, your go-to-market strategy needs to identify three specific people:

1. Who inside that company has the problem you solve, and ideally has it bad enough it keeps them awake at night,

2. Who in the company controls the budget with the funds to deal with the problem, and

3. Who there would be responsible for actually implementing your solution, for putting it to work inside the company.

Let's start with the person who's got the problem. She's the first focus of your attention. She's the one losing sleep wondering what she's going to do about this problem she's got. The more anxious she is, the more she's aware her current system isn't working, the more likely she will welcome your message and listen to what you have to say. Pretty much everything we've been discussing up to now is about her.

The person in pain may not be the person with the budget to fix it.

This is more often true than not, and it's hugely frustrating. Your core audience, the person who's problem you solve, is usually not the one who controls the purse. The bigger the company, the more likely the budget is controlled by someone else. And that's important to you because these two different people almost certainly have different priorities.

The pain experienced by your primary audience is probably not even on the radar for the person who would be the one to pay for it.

This is a dark truth not often discussed. No matter how good your solution is to the overall welfare of the company, the problems you solve are likely not the top priorities for the people you need to get onboard to say "Yes, let's do that."

Because everyone acts on their own personal incentives.

And often, what matters to the person with the budget is not aligned with what matters to the person with the problem. The one in pain wants to fix the problem. The one who controls the budget wants to be careful with limited resources. And he may or may not care about the priorities of the person in pain.

So what can you do to help your case with the person who controls the budget?

The first step to solving a problem is recognizing you have one.

You've already done the first and most important thing, which is to see that this is a decision maker you need to consider as a separate power with their own reasons to do or not do what you want. Once you recognize how important they are, you can work to address their specific concerns just as you worked to influence the person with the core problem. Answer the same questions about the person who controls the money:

- Who is this person?
- What are their individual incentives? How are they rewarded?
- What's their big problem?
- What are they doing about that now?
- How's that working out for them?
- What would they like to do if they could?

Once you have this frame, you can see how you might create a message for the money people who have the power to kill or approve your sale. If you can make their life simpler or easier or more efficient, you have something to say to them.

It always comes down to people.

You need to keep in mind: what matters in messaging to them isn't what's best for the company, but what's best for this person.

Incentives are always personal. People pay attention to what helps them. That's self-centered, but it's not selfishness. It's just how we're all wired to allocate our limited attention spans.

Once you have your strategy for the payer, you can create a communications plan. It can be super simple. Maybe it's a dedicated web page and an email to them. Maybe it's an actual letter. Maybe you speak with them in person at an event or tradeshow. There are hundreds of ways you might put a message to them in a way they might notice.

And your task here is a little easier than it was attracting the attention of your core user. Unless your solution is much more expensive than what they're doing now, you're not asking them to stick their neck out so much, to take a big chance on you. You mostly want them to know that you see them, you understand their part in the process, and you will make sure that whatever resources they allow to flow in your direction is an investment that will pay returns to them, personally.

Who's responsible for implementing your solution?

For a lot of founders and CEOs who want to sell into large organization, it's this third person who too often goes overlooked. They learn too late the power to scuttle their great idea also resides quietly in the hands of the people responsible for keeping the system running.

When you sell to a company, there comes a point when it needs to be put to use, to be integrated with other things the organization has working. This is the job of someone in an operational role, more likely a team of people. They're the ones who make your solution functional.

And they will not want to do it.

"If it ain't broke, don't fix it."

The reason why is clear once you consider who these people are and what are their incentives. These are systems people. They like when things work, and they spend a lot of their time making sure things work well together. This is why we have legacy systems that hang on for years, sometimes decades. The people responsible for making them work don't want to change something that might make the whole operation unstable. They like it when things work, and that mostly means they like it when things stay the same.

At best, your solution is a disruption of their usual process. At worst, it undermines the stability of the overall system they've built. And if your new thing threatens a core function for the people who keep the system running? Unless you've worked to address the specific concerns of these operations people, you will find yourself and your good idea on the outside looking in and wondering what went wrong.

When a good idea was almost strangled at birth

In the early 2000s, a smart young man named Dave married a smart young woman who was a Ph.D. student at Harvard. Dave's wife was writing her thesis on a PC and doing what responsible people did in those days, backing up her work by making CD copies of her hard drive every two or three weeks. One day Dave's wife opened her PC to the blue screen of death, announcing its departure from this earth. And just like that, she lost three weeks of work, gone forever.

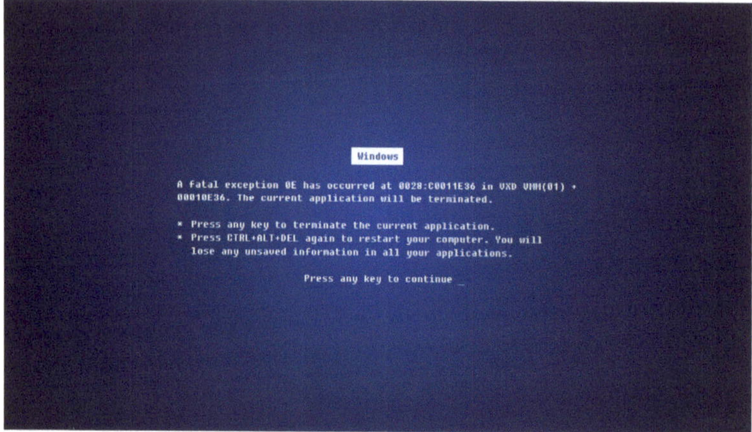

Apologies to those who lived through these times and are now traumatized again.

This made Dave mad, and got him thinking. Why should ownership of the work itself be tied to this particular box? There must be a way to own the data without being dependent upon something as fragile as a PC hard drive.

So Dave created the first automated online backup software that worked in the background. This was at a time when connections were slow, so the software needed to be smart about how and what it backed up. Dave figured out a way to back up just the changes to the files (once the initial big backup had been done), so subsequent backups were small and could be managed in less time, even when broadband internet wasn't available.

Turning the good idea into a company

Dave saw the value in this idea and created a company to sell it, which he called Connected. When Connected took the idea to market they began with big corporations that relied on new information that was created mostly on laptops, often outside the reach of the central servers everyone had then.

These were companies with lots of people on the road, such as sales or consulting firms. When a consultant flew to Detroit to meet with Ford and his PC died during the trip, the consultant and his company had no alternative but to fly him home, set him up with another machine, and send him back out. Now, thanks to Connected, the consultant could pick up a PC at BestBuy, connect online to his home office, and have his contents resurrected remotely.

**The business benefits of automatic backup were obvious to the business people.
But that wasn't enough.**

Finding, and then losing, product-market fit

To the people running these companies, this was a modern-day miracle. Everyone in leadership at consulting firms and sales organizations loved it. Connected started getting sales.

But a strange pattern developed. Connected people would visit a company and would have a great meeting with a prospect who clearly saw the benefit of the new solution. Everyone got excited, agreeing to install Connected on all the company's laptops. Contracts were drawn up. And then, two or three days later, the sale would be canceled.

This happened repeatedly, over and over again. It didn't take much digging to find out why.

Following the meeting, the excited prospect would go talk with their CIO and IT Director. Those talks did not go well for Connected. Where the business prospect saw a chance to protect their most vulnerable and freshest information, the people running IT saw a threat.

When a PC died, it had always been IT's job to recreate it as best they could. If that could be done better by this Connected software, and remotely, IT staffers suddenly became a lot less important to the organization. They were being asked to approve an idea that undermined their value. And they started asking challenging questions.

Where was Connected storing all this sensitive company data? How secure was it? Could the company be sure no one else would have access to it? It wasn't hard to make the whole Connected solution sound unstable and risky. When the IT experts were asked to give their assessment of this new information technology, they came back with strong misgivings, and the sale fell through.

Thankfully, the solution to this problem was just as clear as the objections to the sale.

There's more than one audience to persuade

Connected had done a decent job talking about the business benefits of its solution, but at first they did no job at all with the people responsible for implementation. When operations — in this case, IT — is ignored, it's not hard to predict their opinion of the new idea.

As soon as Connected recognized the information technology experts in these companies — the people who would be responsible for implementing the new solution — as a separate and vital audience, they were able to see that these people have problems and needs distinct from the business side.

So they spoke to both groups simultaneously, with different messages. To the business decision makers, the sale was straightforward: we can ensure you always have a backed-up version of every PC on the edge of your operations, so data formerly at risk would now be safe. The benefit to them was obvious.

To the IT staff, Connected sent a different message: we are going to make you Superman. Before, when someone's PC died, the best IT could do would be to get them a new one, with up-to-date programs but none of their recent files. Now, IT could magically restore the user's PC as it was, including the files they had created away from the home office. And, that PC could be resurrected even without coming home. We gave IT powers they never had before.

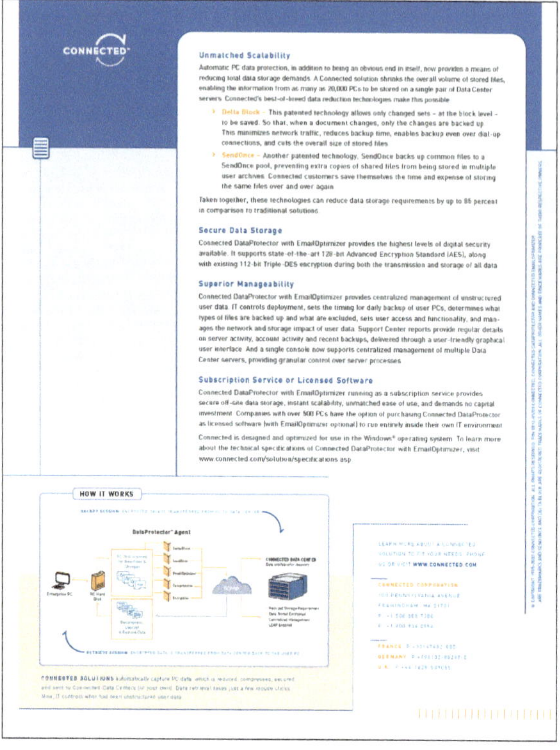

Addressing the needs of people who can kill your solution begins with recognizing their role and their value to the organization. People like to be seen.

The key in this was recognizing that, while the product was the same, the value to the two groups was completely different. The business decision maker was interested in the value of the files, and what Connected could do to protect and recreate them when they were damaged or lost. The IT director was interested in how their role was changing and growing, to protect and restore data that was previously lost forever.

From scrappy startup to titans of industry

Once we were able to speak simultaneously to the concerns of both business people and operations, Connected's sales took off. After a few years they were acquired by the data storage giant Iron Mountain and, in a rare corporate jiu-jitsu, the Connected leadership took over the leadership of Iron Mountain. Connected's leadership team became very rich, and Dave's idea is now the foundation of data protection and storage for many of the world's largest organizations.

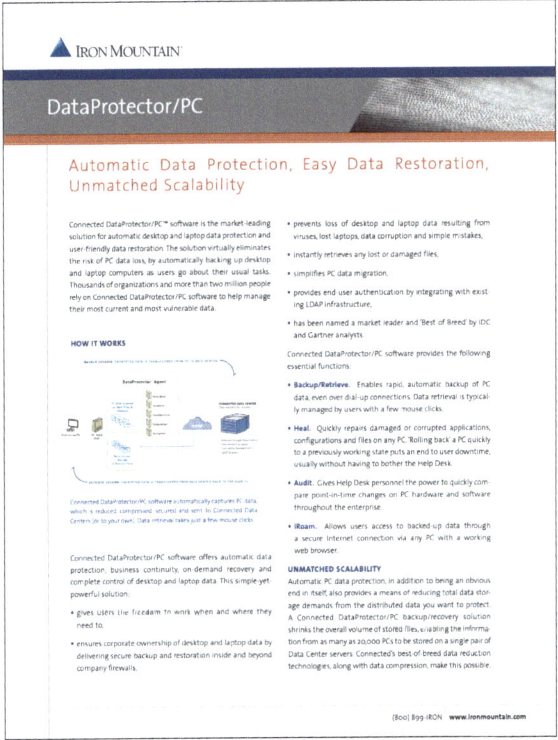

IRON MOUNTAIN

DataProtector/PC

Automatic Data Protection, Easy Data Restoration, Unmatched Scalability

Connected DataProtector/PC™ software is the market-leading solution for automatic desktop and laptop data protection and user-friendly data restoration. The solution virtually eliminates the risk of PC data loss, by automatically backing up desktop and laptop computers as users go about their usual tasks. Thousands of organizations and more than two million people rely on Connected DataProtector/PC software to help manage their most current and most vulnerable data.

HOW IT WORKS

Connected DataProtector/PC software automatically captures PC data, which is reduced, compressed, secured and sent to Connected Data Centers (or to your own). Data retrieval takes just a few mouse clicks.

Connected DataProtector/PC software offers automatic data protection, business continuity, on-demand recovery and complete control of desktop and laptop data. This simple-yet-powerful solution:

- gives users the freedom to work when and where they need to,

- ensures corporate ownership of desktop and laptop data by delivering secure backup and restoration inside and beyond company firewalls,

- prevents loss of desktop and laptop data resulting from viruses, lost laptops, data corruption and simple mistakes,

- instantly retrieves any lost or damaged files,

- simplifies PC data migration,

- provides end-user authentication by integrating with existing LDAP infrastructure,

- has been named a market leader and 'Best of Breed' by IDC and Gartner analysts.

Connected DataProtector/PC software provides the following essential functions:

- **Backup/Retrieve.** Enables rapid, automatic backup of PC data, even over dial-up connections. Data retrieval is typically managed by users with a few mouse clicks.

- **Heal.** Quickly repairs damaged or corrupted applications, configurations and files on any PC. 'Rolling back' a PC quickly to a previously working state puts an end to user downtime, usually without having to bother the Help Desk.

- **Audit.** Gives Help Desk personnel the power to quickly compare point-in-time changes on PC hardware and software throughout the enterprise.

- **iRoam.** Allows users access to backed-up data through a secure Internet connection via any PC with a working web browser.

UNMATCHED SCALABILITY
Automatic PC data protection, in addition to being an obvious end in itself, also provides a means of reducing total data storage demands from the distributed data you want to protect. A Connected DataProtector/PC backup/recovery solution shrinks the overall volume of stored files, enabling the information from as many as 20,000 PCs to be stored on a single pair of Data Center servers. Connected's best-of-breed data reduction technologies, along with data compression, make this possible.

(800) 899-IRON www.ironmountain.com

How often does the startup get acquired and its leadership team end up running the combined organization? Good ideas have power.

B2B marketing succeeds when it addresses the specific needs of each decision maker.

Three steps to keep in mind for anyone who creates a solution for an organization:

1. Find someone inside the company who needs to solve the problem you solve.

2. Then find out who controls the budget for that solution, and then,

3. Who would be responsible for implementing it.

Once you know who they are, you can build a messaging strategy and find ways to reach each group, directing your attention to them individually. Maybe a page on your website and an email campaign is enough. Maybe all the operations people follow the same hashtags on social media. Maybe there's a tradeshow or event just for the IT people in the businesses you're focused on.

When you understand what motivates each of these people — the ones in pain, the ones who control the budget, and the ones in operations who will integrate your solution into everything else they have going on — you have a path to helping them see the benefits of your solution *to them individually*. And then you can win.

It always comes down to people, making decisions based on what matters to them.

— 8 —

CUSTOMERS MOVE TOWARD YOU
STEP-BY-STEP.

You know how some brands seem to explode on the scene all of a sudden? From the outside, it looks like that's how it works. Of course, how it actually works isn't visible on the surface. For pretty much any brand, success is preceded by a series of smaller steps that build to the point where we notice them.

The difference between you and your customers

Every entrepreneur sees the value in what they have to offer, and sees how it can help someone. The problem is that the people we think of as likely customers aren't looking and don't see it. We have to find some way to make it compelling to them.

You have to get out of your own head, forget what you know about what makes your thing so wonderful, and put yourself in the mindset of the people you aim to serve. The ones who know nothing about you yet.

To begin, we can break down your customers' journey into discrete steps, from "They've never heard of us" to "They love us and tell everyone about us". There are eight steps along they way:

1. Not on the same planet.

The more innovative your creation, the harder it is to get anyone to see it.

You can see your future customers from here.

People need a frame to understand where this fits into their lives before they can even consider any fresh idea. In fact, everything we use, every innovation no matter how radical, was first adopted as the direct replacement of something else. Just to take one example: look at your phone.

Why do we call that thing a phone?

How often do you even use it as a phone? Maybe 2% of what we do with it is what we used to do with phones before we got these. The reason why we call them phones is because, when these devices first arrived, they were a direct replacement for the cellular phones we were carrying. Calling this new thing a "phone" gave you an idea of something you could do with it. Of course, once we had them in our pockets the applications multiplied and the world changed. But first, they were adopted as phones.

This is a pattern. Cellular phones began as mobile equivalents to the telephones we once had at our desks and on the walls of our kitchens.

Mom doesn't seem to notice her darlings eating the frosting out of the bowl before it gets onto the cake. Apparently phones, in whatever form, have been wreaking havoc in family life for more than a century.

And, going back, those wired phones were first a direct replacement for an existing technology. Once Alexander Graham Bell won the race for the patent, telephones were used for the same exact tasks as telegraphs. They were put where telegraphs had been, and used at first only for short, direct, urgent messages. The whole "talking on the phone" thing happened only once telephones found their way into homes.

Ever notice how some founders look like straight-up curmudgeons? Alexander Graham Bell here, Thomas Edison, Henry Ford. Startup life is fun, right?

Radical new ideas need a way into the landscapes and mental maps of the people who use them. The quickest path in is one that's already there. Once the new idea gets a foothold it can expand its role, but if it doesn't fit a need the user already has, that never happens.

The problem in attracting attention begins by considering how to fit your creation, the thing you've been working on for years now, into the minds of people who have no idea what your thing even is.

It's not just that they haven't heard of you. What you do may meet a need they don't even realize they have. They can't understand what you've got there until they can connect it to something they need now.

What made Steve Jobs extraordinary was not only what he created, but his ability to get those new ideas into first the minds and then the hands of users.

"People don't know what they want until you show it to them." This was Steve Jobs when he came back to Apple, before he led creation of the iMac (rejuvenating personal computing), the iPod (reshaping how we listen to music), iTunes (how music gets from artists to us, for better or worse), the iPhone (creating mobile computing, redefining the meaning of 'phone', and obliterating entire hardware categories including personal digital assistants like the Palm and pretty much every mp3 player), and the iPad (putting digital tools into places they hadn't been before).

Even if you're not Apple, your original thinking might be a challenge to the people you envision as customers.

The phones we carry around now are infinitely more powerful than those devices that were called 'personal digital assistants', but we still call these 'phones'. The 'phone' label helped ease them into our hands before we knew what they could do.

That slow blink you get when describing your creation to a stranger is them struggling to understand it. At first, your solution may fall into the category of "unknown unknowns", something people have never thought about.

You may want to consider how to ease it into their hands.

2. Unawareness

"Never heard of it." There's some implicit hostility to that answer, which is wired into all of us. It's understandable. There's so much for us to know and do just to get through the day, our default is to reject anything that might upset our system.

Now, as a creator, someone offering something new, this becomes your challenge. The first step to overcoming their resistance is recognizing it's there.

The people you envision as customers have to understand what your thing is before even saying they don't know it, and that's an imposition on their attention. At this point, you own no space inside their heads and they'd like to keep it that way. For them to know your name costs them mental energy they'd rather not exert. "One more thing I don't need" is the default, for every new brand.

This is the toughest nut to crack, and it begins by understanding your future customers' mindset so you can _answer the question they're already asking_. (See Chapter 2.)

3. Aided Recall

"I think I've heard of it," is the next step up, when your brand name rings a little bell inside people's heads. You have made a small dent in their consciousness, which is a testament to whatever you're doing. That took effort on your part. It's a real achievement. And as we know from the world of atoms, it's easier to make a dent if you apply your energy consistently on a focused area.

The path to getting people to recognize your brand is to make them want it before they know why they want it. <u>Attention is not rational</u>. (See Chapter 4.)

4. Unaided Recall

"Yeah, that thing." Ask people to name a brand in your category and see if they mention yours. If more than just a few people in your audience can come up with your name unprompted, you are on your way to a sustainable business. This is the first reliable indicator you are about to make money. If they know you, there's a good chance they'll choose you.

5. Trial

"I tried that thing once." Someone spent money on your thing. To go from unaware to putting down money to pay for what you do is a true achievement. Note that there are four steps on the way to becoming a customer. How many of your buyers went from 'not on the same planet' to paying for your thing in one step? Probably none of them. You brought them along, step by step.

6. Repeat Use

"I use it for _____." This is where your product performance shines. Repeat users found something to like about your thing the first time they used it, enough to come back. You should take a moment to celebrate. You are doing three very difficult things: getting people 1) to notice your creation, 2) to pay for the privilege of using it, and 3) to enjoy the experience enough that they're willing to do it again.

Now you may ask yourself, Why doesn't every user come back? Is this a one-and-done kind of solution? Everlasting Gobstoppers and do-it-yourself vasectomy kits fall into this category. Or is there another occasion when a user might need your thing? Why didn't they use yours the next time? What can you say to them that might tilt them in your direction again, and where might you put that message?

And then, is there something you can do to prod them to tell others about it?

7. Advocacy

"When I'm asked, I tell people about this one." Now you've got a valuable, sustaining brand. When yours is the name that comes up whenever people talk about the need you satisfy, you've got something intangible — your brand — that's worth more than the solution itself.

There is a part of their mind with your name attached to it. Your brand generates market traction.

8. Evangelism

"You have got to try this thing." Among category enthusiasts some brands achieve this peak, when users will do the branding work for you. They like it so much, they will put a dent in *other people's heads* on your behalf. As with every step along this path, the key here is a self-reinforcing message that builds upon something you share with your customers.

Moving up these steps begins by recognizing that there are these distinct steps on the way up and prodding your customers along, one step at a time. If you're clear-eyed about where your customer is along the journey, you have the power to put a message in front of them, right at that moment, that moves them forward and deepens their relationship with you.

Go to market is not a one-time event.

However enthusiastic your customers are, none of them go from unaware to advocacy in one step. Market traction comes from a clear-eyed view of who you're sending your message to, where they are in this journey, and what you might do to get them to the next step. If you skip a step, people can fall off. If you see where you may be overreaching, you might be quick enough to backtrack before you lose them. When you're honest about where someone is and where you can expect to take them next, you can move them toward you.

— 9 —

BUILD YOUR MESSAGE ON
HUMAN TRUTHS.

How do you get people to pay attention when they are trying as hard as they can to ignore you? When they are the targets of a non-stop barrage of 30,000 messages every single day?

How can you convince them you're worthy of their attention?

You can show them something real. Remember, one of the main reasons marketing is largely ignored is because the default assumption is that you're lying.

If marketing is deception, manipulation, deceit, you have an opportunity to create not-marketing, something else worthy of your buyers' attention, by being honest.

Truth is magic.

A friend and colleague of mine once asked me, "But don't you feel badly about using persuasion to influence people? To manipulate them?"

No, I don't feel badly at all. Because effective persuasion isn't manipulation.

Persuasion is alignment.

When we think about the things we choose to do, we know this is true. The brands we come back to again and again, the places we choose to spend our time, the things that feel like "me"resonate because they're aligned with who we are and how we show up in the world.

The same dynamic is what works with what you have to offer and why someone might care about it. It's not manipulation, and it's not a trick. Your prospects give you their attention because there's something about what you've got there that aligns with something about them. Alignment between what you're doing and what your prospects care about.

That's not to say it's easy to do.

The truth is more than just being honest about what your thing does or how it works. It's about connecting with something deeper than the features or functions of your creation, something essential that you share with your prospects.

The truest thing is revealed truth.

These are the truths we know are true but hadn't realized until they're shown to us. When an essential truth is revealed, it has the power to astonish us. Nothing makes us pause our lives to notice something as when someone shows us something we suddenly recognize as true.

That word is instructive: *recognize*. We knew it before and forgot it, and now we are literally RE (once again) COGNIZING (understanding) it again. When we recognize some truth, we are integrating the message with everything else we know.

It's not about the thing.

Better than talking about the thing, sometimes, is to make your message about what your thing is to the person who uses it. There are now more than 4,000 different Lego pieces. This ad only uses two. Lego isn't about the bricks. It's about imagination.

The values behind your creation are closer to the truth than the creation itself.

Dang, this is so good. I've been that guy on that plane with that bag of nuts.

Yes, there's a Harley-Davidson motorcycle in this ad, barely. What makes it effective isn't the motorcycle. The truth at the heart of it is what owners and wannabe owners know about the brand: Harley-Davidson is freedom.

Sometimes the truth is in what your product doesn't do.

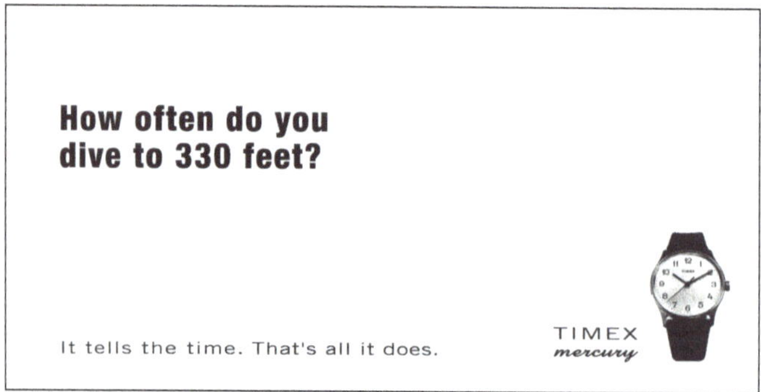

Timex sold a lot of watches when we pointed out that this particular watch does one thing, and one thing only.

Sometimes we see it when it's taken away.

It's not easy to make something as boring as milk into something the cool kids want to drink.

The truth can heal wounds.

KFC ran out of chicken. Not a good day for them. Then they owned it, and turned the chicken crisis into a brand-building opportunity.

85% of your future customers don't care how your solution works.

Remember why you set out to do this in the first place. Why do you love this? How can you distill that feeling to its essence?

Revealed truth is the most persuasive kind.

Put yourself in the mindset of your customers. How do they think about their problem or their need? How is your creation the answer to their question?

How does the problem feel to them, before they think about it?

Parents learn: We're not raising children. We're raising adults who are children at the moment.

"This is not right" is a good place to start.

If you created your solution as a better answer to an important question, that's a great place to make a stand.

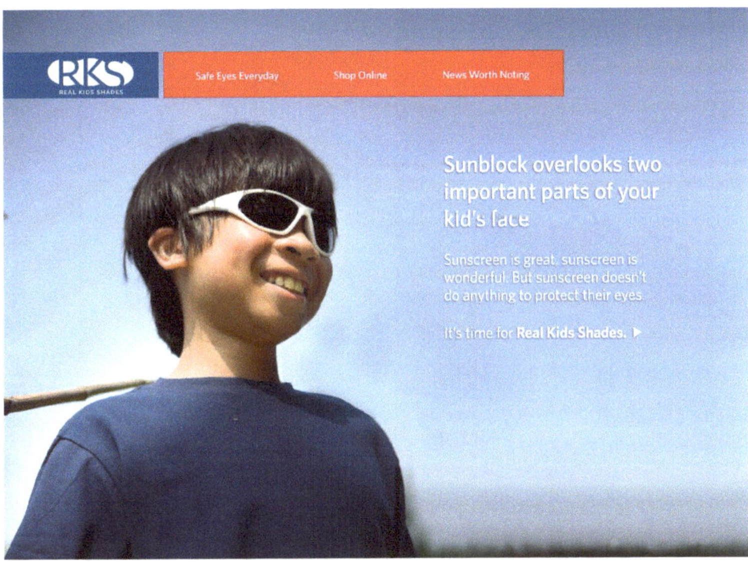

Get back to how you felt when you started up.

A worthwhile company's purpose is to serve its customers' needs. That's why you're doing this. You could have made it just for yourself but you decided you wanted to share your creation with others who can put it to use.

You have something to contribute, something that will make someone else's life better. Those people are persuaded to pay attention when they see how your values match up with theirs.

It's not a trick. Persuasion is alignment.

$$— \; \textbf{10} \; —$$

YOU CAN TELL WHEN YOU'RE GETTING IT RIGHT.

"If it doesn't get measured, it doesn't get managed," we hear. And yes, of course there's truth in that. The only way you know you're moving in the right direction and how fast is to track the change between now and before.

But there's a trap there.

Sometimes you can't measure something directly, so you have to use some kind of proxy to stand in for the thing you want to know. Maybe you can't measure exactly how much people are moved to purchase by a given ad, but if it's digital you can measure how often they click on it. That click is a proxy for motivation to purchase.

It's not the same thing, but it's reasonable to think if they click, they're interested in the product and so they're more likely to want to learn more and to buy what you have to offer, and that grows your business. Right?

Right?

No, not right. That's the trap. That click is not a sale. It may not even be interest in what you have to offer.

The people who make and sell digital tools have done a sleight-of-hand trick here. They've substituted the thing you want — sales — for the thing they can measure — clicks — and convinced you that, since one leads to the other, it's a viable proxy, a reasonable measure of how well you're doing.

Except it's not.

And you know it's not because there's a word for the whole bunch of stuff online that generates clicks and not sales: clickbait. Maybe that cat didn't die in the front part of that video, maybe it did, but clicking on it to find out isn't going to get anyone to buy anything.

The digital world has set up a bunch of proxies for success, and told you that's how this works, that's what you measure. But many of these proxies aren't any kind of viable measure of how you're doing out there.

(If you're interested in the details of digital advertising trickery, Bob Hoffman is just killer on the subject. And he knows what he's talking about.)

So, now what? You're back at Square One?

Let's think this through. You want to grow, right? OK, good. Where does growth come from?

Well, growth comes from sales. The more you sell, the more you're growing.

OK. Where do sales come from?

We can divide sales into two types: 1. You can sell more things to people who already bought something from you, or 2. You can find more people to buy for the first time. How much you can get of each depends in part on what you're selling. It's easier to get people to buy more M&Ms than to buy more houses.

But in either case, sales come from buyers. And you have to get a buyer before you get a repeat buyer. So that sounds right. You need buyers to succeed.

Where do buyers come from?

We know no one tries anything unless they're interested in it first, so interest has to precede buying. So where does interest come from?

This is the challenge: connecting your creation with the interests of your buyers.

As we discussed in Chapter 2, a good way to reframe the Go To Market work is to make your thing look like the answer to a question your intended buyers are already asking.

The bad kind of attention

Attention precedes interest, and not just any attention. Their attention needs to be based on something having to do with why you're here. If you generate attention that isn't aligned with your purpose, you become clickbait. You may remember one pre-digital version of clickbait we talked about in Chapter 4.

Clickbait bullshit started long before the internets. This kind of gratuitous interest has the opposite of its intended effect: by tricking people into paying attention, you're actually teaching your prospects to ignore you from now on.

And this is the problem with measuring clicks. When the proxy gets measured, it becomes the goal. And then the system ends up designed to serve the proxy — clicks — instead of the goal — sales. The whole system becomes corrupted and breaks by building feedback loops around clicks that, in themselves, count for nothing.

Big advertisers know the internet is a shell game.

This is why companies like Procter and Gamble no longer trust or use Google's or Meta's or anyone else's measures of online "performance". The big advertisers figured out that more than 90% of their reported clicks and other digital measurements were generated by bots or invisible ads or some other trickery that fed the clicks counter without having any chance of influencing a human being.

The system of measuring clicks guaranteed this outcome. All the incentives were there for the digital advertising platforms to cheat, and they did. It's built into the system. (Again, see Bob Hoffman for more on this history.)

So what can you do?

Before you can count sales, which you can measure, how do you know you're doing this right?

How to tell if you're headed in the right direction?

And here I have some good news. There is a reliable indicator you're doing this right, and you already know what it is because we all use it as social proof when we make a big purchase: we find out what other people are saying about it.

Word of mouth is the best advertising.

This is why testimonials are so powerful. All the best marketing is expanded word of mouth. When we hear someone enthuse about something, we pay attention, especially when we already trust that person.

Before your sales build, the best indicator that you're on the right track is hearing your message come out of the mouths of your users. When the language you use to promote your thing shows up in the real world, you're getting traction. It tells you three things:

- Your buyers got your message, and absorbed it.

- What you said to them was sticky enough for them to remember it.

- You use language that has become their language to describe your brand. They value what you created and care about it so much, they amplify your message.

When your message — or some version of it — comes out of the mouths of your users, you know you succeeded in making your thing look like the answer to their need.

When they repeat it, they are reinforcing what you're doing, literally increasing the size of the space inside their own heads with your name attached to it, and at the same time laying the seed for a similar space inside the heads of new prospective users.

Your message can be as simple as a single word, and be delivered through media as old as a poster. It does help to get Shepard Fairey to design your poster.

Once there were a bunch of digital music players. Apple won by distilling their message to be as pure and simple as the iPod design. They used to be so good at this.

The simplest form of your message is the name of your brand. MFS Eyewear got a boost when we renamed them

Real Kids Shades, changing the category from a toy to a serious solution to protect children's eyesight.

One of the best lines ever.

BMW changed luxury cars by changing the criteria from cushy elitism to driving performance.

Up to that moment, every ad of every Cadillac showed their cars parked with the owner standing next to it, like it's their house. Only after "The ultimate driving machine" did Cadillac start showing images of their cars in motion.

"Because you're worth it" made L'Oréal the #1 beauty brand and an icon by aligning with women during a powerful cultural moment.

Yogibo's founder made a simple product into a big success thanks to his smarts and hard work and because we got people to ask, "So, what is it then?"

Effective messaging is amplified word of mouth.

The best message is the one that get repeated. It puts an idea into the mind of a possible customer while giving them the language to use when they talk about your creation with others. You're framing your solution for them.

Your good message not only speaks to the people who might use your creation, but to you yourself and your people on the biggest questions:

- Where to focus your energy

- What prospects to put your attention on

- How to allocate your time and money

- Which people to hire

- What kinds of investors you want

Good writing is good thinking.

The advantages of creating and distilling your message extend far deeper than what it takes to get strangers to care about what you've got there. The first and most important audience for any brand message are you and your own people.

They may be your co-creators or employees. They may be your partners, the ones you rely on for key components or support services.

And then it's your supporters, beginning with investors and those who share your vision and want it to succeed.

Be who you are.

Before anyone puts their money or time or attention into what you're doing, they need to understand and align with your vision. When you can communicate that in a compelling way to someone who came in not knowing what you're doing, you are on the right path.

And when you hear your message come back from the mouths of your users, you're on your way to sustaining success.

WHY THIS BOOK

When I didn't die in February 2021, I asked myself what I might do with the time I have now. I'd worked with close to 100 startups at that point (it's more than that now) over more than 20 years, and I'd learned some things founders need to know about how to bring any new creation to market and give it the best chance for success.

I started teaching seminars at the Cambridge Innovation Center and the University of Chicago's Polsky Center for Entrepreneurship, giving away what I'd learned to founders who could put the knowledge to use. Some people asked if there's a book. There wasn't; now there is.

If you're a founder or thinking about it, and want to share what you're doing with me, I'd like to hear from you. You can reach me at bermancreative.com/contact.

I hope you enjoy the book. If you want to get a copy — print or ebook — for someone, drop me a note and I'll help make that happen.

Thanks to the creators who make this world better.